The Bridge of Faith

HIS Glory and

By TK Hinkle

Carmel Clay Public Library Attn: Brian Bobbett Blessings! TK Hinkle

1

The Bridge of Faith

Copyright © 2024 by TK Hinkle

ISBN: 9798873572670

All rights reserved no part of The Bridge of Faith book may be reproduced or transmitted in any form or by any means, printing, electronic or mechanical, including photocopying, recording, or saving any information storages, Al, technology of today and to be invented, retrieval system, without permission in writing from the author TK Hinkle.

Scriptures marked KJV are taken from the KING JAMES VERSION (KJV): KING JAMES VERSION, public domain

Scriptures marked NIV are taken from the NEW INTERNATIONAL VERSION (NIV): Scripture taken from THE HOLY BIBLE, NEW INTERNATIONAL VERSION ®. Copyright© 1973, 1978, 1984, 2011 by Biblica, Inc.™. Used by permission of Zondervan

Dedication:

I would like first to offer love, give thanks, and bestow all of the glory to my Savior, my Lord, Jesus Christ: my hands, Jesus, your power. I love and honor you!

To my middle son, who, physically, emotionally, and mentally, lived out a fierce tragedy that no one should ever have had to endure, and no parent should ever have to witness. To all the public service first responders and medical staff that so bravely carried the burden in aiding to save his life.

Lastly, and of course, not least, my loved ones, friends, and employer, who waited back home for months while I did what I had to do: be with one of my children to the end.

A Special Thank You to:

Denise Pass, for your patience, teaching, time, and being a great friend.

GW Tolley and the knowledge you have placed into your book, "What is STOPPING YOU from Self-Publishing: You have a book idea and now what?" Also, for your time invested and for believing in me.

About the Author TK Hinkle

TK was born in a small midwestern town in Indiana. She graduated mid-term, and the intended purpose was to enroll immediately after in a nearby business college. Still, quickly after graduating, she received news that the funds were unavailable, so she decided to start her own family. The following June, soon after her May graduation ceremony, she married her first husband, and just months later, she gave birth to her first child, a daughter. The decades after would progress to four more children and two more marriages. She has now been honored to have six grandchildren to call her own and is still located in midwestern Indiana, where she serves her Lord, loves her family, and attends church.

She has always believed in the Almighty God (the God of Abraham, Isaac, and Jacob), but the relationship through salvation with Jesus Christ that she was unaware of came much later in life. She had only attended church sporadically on various special occasions throughout her life. She admits to many years of poor choices that led her down a path of destruction and ultimately, found herself in deep sorrow, face down on the floor of her home, wailing out to God to take over her life, confessing she was not worthy to do it on her own any longer. As a result of this profound encounter, He (GOD) instantaneously and supernaturally answered that distressed prayer through deliverance in April 2008.

After years of submerging into her bible, extensive prayer, and sharing the gospel, she has a flourishing relationship with her Lord and Savior.

Would her faith withstand the test laid before her as true to life events unfold? She found herself in the deepest valley she had ever known. Could her Savior prove to be so faithful?

Table of Contents

Foreword

"Tonna's book is raw and real, a testimony from a mother's heart conveying in a conversational style what every mom dreads, yet instilling the eternal hope that carried her through in her darkest hours. As someone who has watched Tonna deepen in her faith as she served in Seeing Deep Ministries, it is a joy to see her use her hardest moment to bring God glory and serve others with her story."

> — Denise Pass, M.A. Biblical Exposition, Author of Make Up Your Mind Book, and Study Guide and Shame Off You, speaker and founder, Seeing Deep Ministries

Denise Pass and I at her Shame Off you book launch

True Story

Chapter 1 Don't Freak Out

It was a typical day at the factory where I worked; it was a Wednesday, the first day of June 2016. It was approximately 9 a.m. and the plastics plant I worked at produced concentrated plastic pellets. I had worked in the shipping department for the last 17 years, and my title at the time was forklift operator. On this particular day, when I had finished with some work orders and went to our receiving office to inquire about more of them, I saw my husband, Charles, and my youngest son, Chace, walking through our shipping department door. At first glance, I thought it would be a pleasant surprise visit, and I was gazing at them, but I was still a little dumbfounded as to wondering why they were there, as it was 9 a.m. and not closer to lunchtime. So, I asked in an excited but mixed with a puzzled tone: "Hey there! What are you two doing here?"

They just looked at each other, not knowing how to tell me and trying to muster all of the composure and courage they could. Chace walked around the corner and then my husband spoke up. His hands extended out in front of him towards me, and as he was calmly warranting me, all was fine, he told me twice that I would need to remain calm, and I said "Okay" with a slow and questionable look. He now continues with a reluctant but stern voice, "Now," he says (pauses), "don't freak out." Stretching out this word exceptionally long and nodding yes, I say, "Ooookaaaaay" (then a pause). While I answered slowly and cautiously, it resulted in terror because I now realize how weighty this news has become and that my world will no longer be "normal."

Again, he proceeded to tell me the rest of the message he had quickly visited to deliver. "Sammy has been in an accident." (He is my middle son. He was 23 then.)

So, I stayed as calm as he had directed. No need to get hysterical for nothing, right? My eyes are glued to his lips, as I do not want to miss a word of what he is trying to tell me. Sammy is the fourth child of five of my own, and throughout his life, he has kept me highly skittish with his many emergencies.

So, somewhere between staying calm because I have been through this before and trying to stay calm because obviously, I was too soon finding out that nothing of this magnitude had ever happened to him. I, once again, say, with still terrified eyes and a long and slow "okay." These were one-word questions and not answers because of the uncertainty; I didn't know how to answer them yet. Then Charles says, "Sammy has been life-flighted" (emergency helicopter). Still with his guarding hands out in front of him and profoundly serious face. He said, "Now, go and grab your things; we have a long drive to the hospital."
Still nodding yes and with a faint and crackling voice, as I try to envision what I was about to witness in my mind's eye, I again answer with an "Okay."

My heart sank deep into my belly. I felt like a punch to my stomach, karate-chopped in the throat and slapped across the face. I hope this is descriptive enough for you, my reader. It is just that my very being, my soul, was shaken so mightily with those few small words, "he has been life-flighted," that I couldn't breathe and only scantily speak. My thinking went amiss. I stopped eating for at least three days. It is hard to eat when your esophagus feels padlocked. I could not even get melted ice down it, and worst of all, I couldn't even pray.

Romans 8:26 (KJV) Likewise the spirit also helpeth our infirmities: for we know not what we should pray for as we ought: but the Spirit itself maketh intercession for us with groanings which cannot be uttered.

Chapter 2   Freaking Out

When it was time for the departure from my work to the hospital, I opened the office door, peeked my head inside, and announced I had to leave now, as my son had been in an accident and life-flighted and to please inform my supervisor on duty I am going.

The walk to the locker room to retrieve my belongings felt like ten miles away. My legs felt so weak and trembly. In reality, it was only about a minute. While irrationally gathering my items, I tried to recall what I needed but wanted to dart out the door without anything. So, while walking out the door at a swift pace, across the parking lot to our vehicle, I was thinking, don't freak out, okay, freak out. Don't freak out; okay, freak out. Hurry! No need to hurry. Hurry! No need to rush. I was so confused I could not get there fast enough.

When we hopped in the van, we started the long 2-hour journey to the hospital where they had taken my son. The trip seemed more like 12 hours instead of 2. I still tried to pray, but I could not get anything to come out but only some scripture. I just kept looking around out the windows, speechless and teary-eyed. Trying to be brave, I would turn around every few miles and look at my youngest son, Chace, in the back seat. Then I would frantically gaze out the window to search for Sammy truck at the accident sight. I just needed to see it. I just needed to know; maybe it would have made things more real. After all, I felt as though I were in a nightmare and hoped it was only a nightmare and I would wake up at any moment. I could barely breathe. When the floodgates had finally opened, and the tears started streaming down my face, I had begun to hyperventilate. Needing air, I would tell my husband to pull over. I wanted to get out and walk around to regain composure and some fresh air for what felt like a budding panic attack.

I used to have them in High School, so I knew what was happening and how to handle it. But then, remembering that time was of the essence, I would say, "Oh, never mind, just keep going. I need to get there as soon as possible." Then, I started talking to Jesus. I was reciting what scripture I could concentrate on. At one point, I had finally asked my husband, "Where is his truck?" referring to my son's truck, "Did they have to cut him out of it?" Where did it happen?" In my mind, I was recalling all the life-threatening accidents where the injured victims needed the jaws of life to cut them out. I wanted to know more about what had happened and where it had happened. "Have we passed it already?" I would periodically ask these questions.

As I said, Sammy had been in numerous accidents, mainly involving vehicles, but also other things. I had a terrible fear that it was eventually going to cause him his death. So, this is where my thoughts were stuck since I had first learned of him being life flighted.

My husband finally replied as he looked at me, worried and puzzled, "No, Tonna," he said, "he fell from a bridge while at work." So, my mind immediately went to the fact that he had driven his truck off the bridge at work. I was so stuck on the fact he was in his vehicle that when I had initially heard the word accident, that's where my thoughts went and stayed. I think my husband finally understood what I was thinking, and he told me that Sam, himself, had fallen off, but not while he was in his truck.

So, his poor, fragile body had hit the ground with no protection but only a hard hat. It was like hearing about the accident all over again. I had finally started to grasp the severity of this situation. I knew I needed prayer. He needed prayer. I knew I still needed to pray and sensed still being so shocked that I could not. So, I started calling people in my contacts list that I knew would pray. I tried as calmly as possible, phoning them one by one and saying, "This is Tonna; Sammy had been in an accident; he has been life-flighted, and I do not know any more than that. Please pray for him." They would say, "Yes, I will be praying," and we would hang up.

I felt utterly useless but, obviously, not hopeless. I turned to the back seat and asked my son Chace to sing how great our God is, and we began to sing. I never knew just how valuable and comforting singing would be.

Soon, my phone rang, and I answered. It was my youngest daughter, Kensi. I was so grateful to hear her voice, although it did not seem like it because of my uncontrollable crying. She speaks with a crackling and faint voice. "Mom?" I responded with tears rolling down my face, barely talking. "Yes?" "It's Kensi." she said. I could not speak. I could not answer at all, just a bunch of crying, breathing hard, and trying to catch my breath. She finally put my oldest daughter, Randi, on the phone, and again I heard, "Mom? It's Randi." "Are you on your way to the hospital?" "Yes." She speaks again and says, "Everything is going to be okay. I've called the hospital, and they said they have medical personnel praying over Sammy while treating him as we speak."

I have to say that it was very reassuring to learn that they were praying over him. While I was gathering prayers from others and singing about how great our God is, our God had some of His people laying hands on Sammy and praying over him, working through their hands spiritually and physically. Something that I was unable to do even if I had been there and our mighty Lord knew it; of course, He did. That was the first recollection of hearing from God in this journey so far. I had been hearing from Him already when I was calling on people to pray, and I did not realize that the LORD was guiding me to do so because of the shock I was in. I had been blindsided and was trying to make sense of it all. It's like being hit over the head, seeing stars, and trying to shake off being disoriented, just like we have seen in cartoons. Come to realize it later, both of my daughters told me he had fallen, but I just didn't comprehend it.

I had been telling Jesus that I could not pray. I did not know what else to do if I could not pray but sing, call upon others, and ask them to pray. I could not believe it. The medical staff were praying over my son! A part of me knew Jesus was in control of all of this already, which, in my mind's eye, I knew; I could not yet recognize the massiveness of it.

Everything had become tangible as if Jesus were in the flesh and I could physically touch Him. The Lord reminded me a few days later how I had sown seeds of prayer for years prior because every time I heard sirens, I prayed for all involved. The family members, the ones behind the wheels of the vehicles as well as the ones they were driving to help. Only God.

After my daughters and I had discussed a few things, like where I was and where we were going they told me there was a mix-up about the facility where they had taken him, of which I was unaware. It seems they were in route to one emergency facility but had to reroute to another because of an approaching storm that would be in their path. I also recall being informed that the emergency facility he was first taken to diagnosed his injuries to be greater than what they were equipped for and sent him on through a life-flight. Thankfully, they were able to send him to a facility in his field of injuries.

To conclude the phone call with my daughters, we said we loved each other and hung up. I could then pray this simple prayer, "Lord, please keep him alive until I get there, amen!"

Wow! That sounds so small compared to such a colossal circumstance. But I meant it. At that point, I wanted to tell him how much I loved him and say goodbye if the Lord had decided to call him home. It was not what I wanted, but this is a fallen world. People die! Our loved ones die, whether we are prepared to say goodbye or not. It is not up to us. We are not in control. Ultimately, Jesus says when it is time to take our next breath and it might just be our last one. I also wanted my other four children there with me and my grandchildren, where I could hold them and tell them I love them. I talked with my other son, and he wanted to come, but was just too traumatized to see his younger brother in that condition. He needed a little time and then he soon came to see him.

We can only ask in prayer for His will to possibly spare our pain of losing a loved one and or request to please let them be okay. Being rattled, I still knew who to go to. Who I could depend on. Who I could trust. Who was in charge and who could answer my weak little prayer. I soon discovered that my prayer was not so weak or so little at all. I pray the Lord always reminds me to come to Him.

Psalm 23 (KJV) The LORD is my shepherd; I shall not want. He maketh me to lie down in green pastures: He leadeth me beside the still waters. He restoreth my soul: He leadeth me in the paths of righteousness for his name's sake. Yea, though I walk through the valley of the shadow of death, I will fear no evil: for thou art with me; Thy rod and thy staff they comfort me. Thou preparest a table before me in the presence of mine enemies: Thou anointest my head with oil; my cup runneth over. Surely goodness and mercy shall follow me all the days of my life: And I will dwell in the house of the LORD forever.

Isaiah 41:10 (KJV) "Fear thou not; for I am with thee: be not dismayed; for I am thy God: I will strengthen thee; yea, I will help thee; yea, I will uphold thee with the right hand of my righteousness."

The bridge

16

Chapter 3   Emergency Entrance

Finally arriving at the hospital in the rerouted location, we searched for the emergency entrance because I believed he was in the emergency room. I did not realize they had already moved him to his own ICU (intensive care unit) room. My husband and youngest son dropped me off at the doors then went to park the car. The double doors slid open, and I walked in, looking around for the desk to get directions. I was in so much confusion. I needed someone to talk to and hold my hand to guide me. I found someone and stopped to inquire about the proper information.

"Hello!" I said, "I'm TK, and my son, Sammy Cooper, has been life-flighted here. Can you please tell me what room he is in?" Desk personnel #1- "Yes, ma'am. You will need to walk through that door right there." She was pointing off to her right at a door that led to the emergency rooms. I responded, "Thank you!" and journeyed to find my son.

I approached another desk with receptionist #2 and stopped to ask her the same question. First, she speaks up and asks, "Hello! May I help you?" I said, "Yes. Thank you! I am TK, and my son is Sammy Cooper. He was life-flighted here, and I am looking for him." She responds, "Oh, yes! The chaplain is waiting right over there because he is expecting you."

What! I exclaimed in my head. Fear and shock, and I am sure my eyes were huge. My knees were weak. Why is the chaplain waiting on me? What has happened? These questions were rolling around through my mind. The chaplain could only mean one thing. He had died and/or was going to die at any second. I was terrified at what I was going to hear next. I knew they had to see the terror in my eyes. I felt like I was in another dimension, like a nightmare, and none of it was real except the pain in my heart.

I approached the chaplain, and he spoke up to say, "Hello!" He introduced himself, and with his hand extended, he shook my hand. "Your son is upstairs in the ICU trauma unit. Follow me, and I will take you up there." I thankfully but squeamishly answer, "Okay. But I must wait a few seconds on my husband and son as they are right behind me." Things were quickly going further south for me, which was not good.

My other son, Chace, and my husband arrived in a matter of seconds, and we started the journey to Sam. As we began our walk down the hospital corridor, the chaplain turned away from me and began taking steps, he again said, "Follow me. "Okay," I answered. We all four single-filed down the hallway. I was second in line behind the chaplain. I was still trying to understand what I would see and how I would react. What exactly was going to happen? I kept hearing the chaplain's footsteps echoing like we were watching a scary movie in an empty hospital. Clomp! Clomp! Clomp! The sound of the heels of his black dress shoes was deafening as my nightmare unfolded. I will never forget that.

We reached the elevators, and I must tell you I do not ride elevators, especially in my emotional state. They do not sit well with me in the first place. I was already feeling as though I was suffocating and just wanted to throw up or run away or something to feel better. But that "better" would not come for many days, especially not in the form of an enclosed elevator. I stopped the chaplain and said, "Oh! I am deeply sorry, but I don't do elevators." I think possibly the already overwhelming fear was telling me that an enclosed elevator would be harder for me to breathe. He was genuinely nice about it and responded, "It's okay. Not a problem. I can take you around the corner to the stairs."

So, we rounded the corner and reached the stairway. Thankfully, the ICU was only on the second floor. As we approached my son's room, the chaplain stopped slightly ahead of me and held up his hand for me to walk into the room first. I could not believe my eyes as I walked through the door. There lay my beautiful, perfect son with a neck brace, tubes down his throat, chest tubes, wires from a port, and a catheter. He was gasping to breathe like a fish out of water. He was unable to communicate, and his eyes were closed. He kept reaching out into the air like a baby does when it thinks it is falling. His legs would draw up near to him. I could not grasp what was going on, but it had me in so much emotional pain. The tears were uncontrollable and gushing.

Sammy father was in the room also. We had ended our relationship when Sammy was only four years old. So much guilt and shame had landed on my shoulders. I was so sorry for everything, and I do mean everything. There were times when there were thoughts that this may be something I deserved because his father and I were no longer together. But the Lord reminded me this is not a punishment. His dad was hurting as well. He was at a loss for words, shocked, and tears in his eyes. Overall, his dad and I have maintained a cordial relationship.

So perplexed at first sight, I was still incapable of praying. All I could do was shake my head and cry. I grabbed my son's hand and said, "Sam, it's momma bear," which was his name for me. "I am here with you. Hang on Sam, hang in there, they are taking care of you." Oh, Lord Jesus, this was nauseating to witness. He was reaching out, grasping for something to hang on to. Over and over and over again. He was breathing so rapidly but shallowly, and his body was locking up so tight. His eyes were closed, but he was still trying to communicate. No one knew what he was trying to say. No one knew what he was trying to do. I often wonder if he were having seizures by the way he was pulling his legs up towards his chest and grabbing on so tight to anything that he could as he reached out with his hands. He nearly broke my hand. I discovered a few years later that this is what they call brainstorming (or neurostorming that often occurs after a severe head injury. Kind of like a short circuit). I was weeping. Exactly as you see in the movies, there was no helping him, and he was slowly dying but very tragically. I would later learn that he may have felt like he was falling repeatedly. No one knows and he has no memory of it. (Nowadays, he has mentioned having recurring dreams of falling.) For hours on end, this was the scenario. It was relentless. We would think he was calming down, and then this attack would resurface. Why? Just why? When I felt I could not do this any longer, he lay still and seemed to rest for a while. At one point, I was holding on tight to his hand, talking to him, telling him how much I loved him, and saying how sorry I was for all the whippings I had given him when he was little. He did not really know how bad he was; he was just a little boy. Growing up, I was disciplined with whippings and thought that was the correct answer. But no blame on anyone, we all do what we know at the time.

I would just lay over him with tears falling from my eyes, and they were running down his hand and soaking his hospital gown. I was completely and utterly broken.

At another point, it seemed like a breakthrough when he was trying to talk to me. Like he knew it was me, but his eyes were still closed. He moved his lips like he was talking, and I said frantically, "Sam? What is it? What are you trying to say?" And he just mouthed the word momma. That did me in. I answered, kind of hysterically, I said. "Yes, Sam! It is mom. What are you trying to say? You are at the hospital. You had an accident. But they are doing everything they can to help you." He laid his head down, and that was it for a short while, as if he could rest for a bit.

Well, there it was. The Lord had kept him alive until I had arrived. I could tell him how much I loved him, which I did many times. I do not even know if he heard me, but I needed to say it, and I am so thankful that the Lord allowed me to do so. Now, what to pray for next?

Mark 11:24 (KJV) Therefore I say unto you, What things soever ye desire, when ye pray, believe that ye receive them, and ye shall have them.

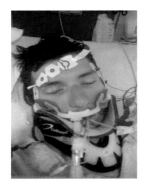

Chapter 4   An Emotional Rollercoaster

Not only did I have to face the pain of my own emotions, but I also had to see the pain in everyone else's eyes. The looks on the faces of his father and his relatives. The pain in the eyes and on the faces of his siblings, my four other children. The grief in the eyes and on the faces of my family members. On the faces of friends, his and mine. On the medical staff. On the police officer who used CPR to revive him. It was like a funeral. All in disbelief and despair. It seemed as though I was in and out of reality.

Believing he was going to make it and then seeing him struggle to gasp for each breath of air and talk to the doctors had me on an emotional rollercoaster. That will mess with your mind, let me tell you. Then, I had to come to terms with it and ask myself, what would he be like if he did make it? Brain dead but alive? Awake but not able to communicate? Would he walk, talk, eat, and breathe on his own? The most devastating was, would he even know me? I knew God had a plan, just like HE always does. But what was it? Why had He brought him back to life? Why had He saved him up to this point? Did He do it for me because I prayed? Because his dad prayed? Because hundreds or even thousands prayed? Or, ultimately, so we could all cry out to Him for help? Maybe all of the above. I only know one thing for sure: He did it all for His glory. He saved him for a purpose, His purpose. We now need to search for His purpose, and this is how I use it for His glory.

Romans 8:28 (KJV) "And we know that all things work together for good to them that love God, to them who are the called according to his purpose."

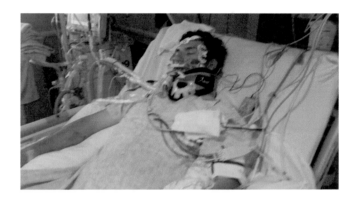

Sammy in ICU, how I first saw him

Chapter 5   No Surgery, No Medicine, but God

While still in the ICU at the rerouted facility, Sammy father repeatedly left the room, unable to watch the horror unfolding before us. He said I was much better at dealing with these things than he was. The only difference I could see was that I sought a supernatural intervention from the Lord. He could have been as well, but just in private. Every night for a couple of weeks, it felt like it was still the first night, just so raw. But I knew had Jesus. So, I had hope. Although, I cannot say I had an emotional handle on it because, in human terms, it was a shock. One of the chaplains, who was also a counselor, told me I was experiencing a form of PTSD. That is a real thing in events such as this. It happens to the loved ones—the result of a severe traumatic experience. Emotional rollercoaster. A sense of an earth-shaking event that doesn't stop shaking. It caused sleep deprivation and loss of appetite.

Shortly after I had arrived, the doctors came in with some bleak news for me. The pulmonologist who treated Sammy lungs would be the first to speak with me. He introduced himself, "Hello, I'm the doctor treating you son, Sam." He had his hand out to shake mine and had an accent. He continued speaking to explain that three-quarters of Sammy right lung was irreparably damaged, all of the ribs on his right side broken, and the right collar bone entirely broken into. He added that there was nothing they could do. No surgery, no medicine. The ex-rays would reveal even more grim news: the left lung had been punctured. A few broken ribs on the left side had made this newly discovered hole. He went on explaining that he had to place chest drainage tubes in on both sides. All of this had explained the reason it was exceedingly difficult for him to breathe on his own, actually impossible, even on life support he was struggling. They eventually put the boots on him to prevent his feet from laying down and having foot drag.

The doctor also explained that he bronched (cleaned out) the right lung, but he could do nothing with the left one. He wasn't happy with the choice he had made for his right lung because he would never typically choose to do that procedure to a lung with that much tissue damage. That was just not the proper procedure at all for this kind of trauma. He was shaking his head in grief, but then, later, he said how that proved to be the right thing to do because it helped him to breathe a bit better. He didn't completely understand it, except that it could have only been God. He said he had a son the same age as Sammy and did not know how he would handle it emotionally if it were his child. He had so much empathy for me. He would later tell me that he felt as though his head ended up in the clouds because he knew of nothing else to try. He contacted all qualified colleagues he could think of, asking if they might have some guidance for something else to try.

Though, at that time, he had no idea how high he was in the clouds, Jesus was working through him, in other words, but about his professional contacts, no one could give him any answers. They all were in agreement they had done all they knew. He also said that he had everyone in his office praying for Sammy and the only thing we needed was for God himself to come down from heaven and reach into Sammy chest and operate on his lungs because that is all there is. I told the doctor, then that is what I am standing on! God.

Genisis 2:7 (KJV) And the LORD God formed man of the dust of the ground and breathed into his nostrils the breath of life; and man became a living soul.

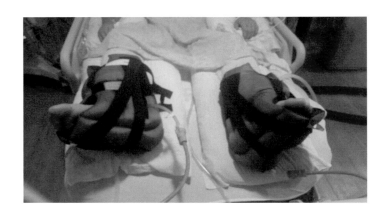

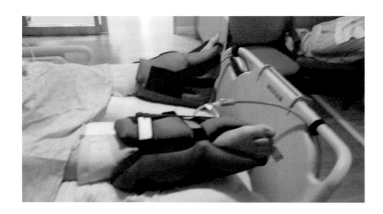

Chapter 6   Chopped Liver

The next doctor I spoke with was the trauma surgeon. Could things possibly get any worse, I thought? I didn't dare ask that question, but, oh yes, they most certainly could and did. The doctor proceeded to explain to me that on a scale of one to five, the prognosis of Sammy liver rated at a four, with five being fatal. The description of Sammy liver injury was as if you would drop an egg on the floor, and it would crack open in many places. That is what his liver looked like. I was really starting to see the "not so pretty picture" being painted of my son's insides. He also regretted to inform me that there was nothing he could surgically do for a liver with this kind of injury. He also regretted to inform me the only thing they could do for an injured liver such as this was to lay him flat. But guess what? Because of his lungs, he could not lay flat. He needed to be elevated because of his severely damaged lungs. There was nothing that could be done, not for the broken bones and not for the damaged organs. When they tested his blood, they found that he needed two pints. His dad and I both signed for him to receive it. After a couple of days, ultimately and thankfully, Sammy would not need any more blood; that did not mean he would be okay; it only meant his liver was slowly regaining function. Praise the Lord!

Ezekiel: 3-5 (KJV) 3 And he said unto me, Son of man, can these bones live? And I answered, O Lord God, thou knowest. 4 Again he said unto me, Prophesy upon these bones, and say unto them, O ye dry bones, hear the word of the Lord. 5 Thus saith the Lord God unto these bones; Behold, I will cause breath to enter into you, and ye shall live:

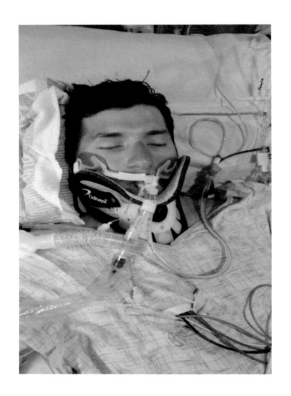

Sammy's ICU room in a coma

Chapter 7   More Than Meets the Eye

Now, for the problem with his right eye. They were concerned with it because it was not reacting to light appropriately. When he had fallen, his head hit the railroad tracks. He had his hard hat on, but it popped off and went flying. The muscle to his right eye was damaged, and the TBI (Traumatic Brain Injury) was discovered with the MRI (Magnetic Resonance Imaging}. It was a brain shearing where different areas of his brain were torn, like in the shaken baby syndrome, which is how they described it to me. I was just devastated. I was so sick. I could not believe my ears; it was bad news after bad news. He had to wake up and be okay; he just had to. I would not accept that he may never wake up and if he did, that he might not function on his own. I had to believe that Jesus had a purpose to have brought him this far.

From death to life. From a lady witnessing the fall to a police officer bringing him back with CPR and all of the thousands of prayers going up. This was devastating news once again. I could not help but ask God, why? I told Him I had been walking so close to Him for so long; why? Why my son? God! How could you let this happen to my son? I honestly, had become angry with God. He immediately responded to my questions because He is faithful and forgiving. He said that the enemy had caused him to stumble but that He would turn it around for His glory and our good. I heard Him loud and clear. That would hold me over until the following grim news I would receive. Still, praised God!

Genesis 50:20 (NIV) You intended to harm me, but God intended it for good to accomplish what is now being done, the saving of many lives.

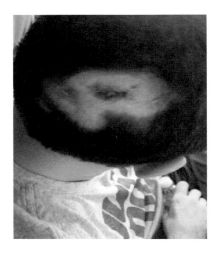

This image is of the injuries to his head

Chapter 8   Overflowing

My pastor was the first to call me since I had arrived at the hospital. He said that the congregation would hold a prayer vigil that evening. My heart was overflowing. That was yet another massive word of encouragement. Every day for the first four weeks, I could not believe the amount of people sending prayers. It was all over social media. There was a Go-Fund-Me page and other fundraisers for his benefit. People were showing up from all over. The corporates from the company where he was a member and employed. The liaisons are from the employer's insurance company. I had many friends, family members, and my phone was blowing up from calls where people wanted to pray. They told me they prayed for him at church and put on various prayer chains. I read scripture over him, and when I was not doing that, I asked others to pray over him. The Lord is so awesome, though. He would send a chaplain into the room whenever I needed prayer to ask me if I needed anything. I would, of course, always answer, with bewilderment and relief at the same time, something like this: "Yes! I was praying for the Lord to send someone in to pray. I am just at a loss for words right now." "Yes! Please pray with me over him."

As I mentioned previously, so many friends were concerned about Sam. The waiting room was always full of people. There were so many in and out of his room. They were waiting to hear if he was going to be ok. I was very thankful that so many cared as much as they did. They brought food, cards, and gifts, gave money, and raised money to help cover costs not included in the insurance. Also, to help with Sammy bills.

A co-worker working next to him saw him fall first-hand and tried reaching down to grab and save him from falling. He said he tried so hard but could not reach him, causing him to be distraught. I could see it on his face, in his eyes, and hear it in his voice. He stayed for as long as he could handle it emotionally, many hours. He has no idea how much being there and explaining a snip from his perspective had helped me. It was a sense of understanding what happened instead of trying to visualize it. Prayerfully, someday, I will have the opportunity to speak to all who were involved in any way. Other co-workers had come to console me and help me however needed. Another one that Sammy often carpooled with brought me the keys to Sammy truck, his wallet, and Sammy bib overalls, which were cut off of him when he fell. Things that I was not even thinking of at that time. So thankful for them as well.

As people were calling and wanting to know how he was doing, I was also overwhelmed with support from other brothers and sisters in Christ. Crowds arrived at the hospital as though it were a funeral and pay their respects, looking like defeated warriors returning from the battlefield. Emotionless, perplexed, exhausted, and not knowing what to expect. They did not know what they would see or say, like the aftermath of war, as you see in the movies. I had a vision of the war films that I have watched in the past. I, however, unlike the visitors, had already been engaged in a war, a spiritual war as well an emotional one. Not knowing what God had in store, I was hanging on for dear life.

I knew He was orchestrating something massive, to a scale I personally had never seen. I am genuinely thankful for all who cared enough to attend and even the phone calls.

Knowing how many people loved my son meant so much to me. I am so grateful that the Lord would have me surrounded by others who believed in Him.

Every morning and every evening, they would have a moment of prayer over the hospital intercom. I would stop, no matter what, and pray along with. That was so comforting as well. I knew I was in a place that was full of prayers, fellow believers, and just so full of Godliness. The Lord knew that was exactly where I needed to be, where Sammy needed to be—surrounded by the very essence of Jesus Christ. I sensed Him in every moment.

Philippians 4:11-13 (KJV) 11Not that I speak in respect of want: for I have learned, in whatsoever state I am, therewith to be content. 12I know both how to be abased, and I know how to abound: everywhere and in all things I am instructed both to be full and to be hungry, both to abound and to suffer need. 13I can do all things through Christ which strengtheneth me.

The bib overalls the first responders cut off Sammy

33

Chapter 9   Seeing What Mary Saw

Despite everyone's best efforts, Sammy developed pneumonia, as if his lungs could not get any worse. He was fighting the life support equipment, and it was to the point where they could not increase the oxygen; it was at the max. So here was just another roadblock, or was it? There were many pulmonary experts and respiratory therapists in and out of the room, and they were suctioning his bronchial tubes as often as they could. They were exceptionally great at their job. They took excellent care of Sam, but finally, they had to do something different, and they decided to give him a drug to help him relax so he wouldn't fight anymore, and that was the hardest decision for me to make. I was again fearful of what and why and that maybe they were not telling me everything maybe just to protect my feelings or something. To give him this drug would mean to put him in a medically induced coma or actually, keeping him in one he was in only relaxed. They would now need Sams's exact weight and exact height. So, they already knew his weight because the bed he was in had a tare weight, but to get his height, they would need to measure him from a tall man's fingertip across his chest to his other tall man's fingertip. As they documented the measurements required, I stood observing at the foot of the bed. I watched as they grabbed his left wrist and pulled it tight to straighten his arm, while another team on the other side of the bed pulled his other arm in the opposite direction. Just like in the game of Tug of War, only then done with a rope. Then, they ran the tape measure from fingertip to fingertip and got his height. Standing at the foot of that bed and watching from that angle, I felt a drop of Mary's pain, Jesus' mother. I started saying The Lord's Prayer: *Matthew 6:9-13 (KJV) After this manner therefore pray ye: Our Father which art in heaven, Hallowed be thy name. Thy kingdom come, Thy will be done in earth, as it is in heaven. Give us this day our daily bread. And forgive us our debts, as we forgive our debtors. And lead us not into temptation, but deliver us from evil: For thine is the kingdom, and the power, and the glory, forever. Amen.*

That was so moving to me and even encouraging. I had received a revelation. I instantly realized that it could have been much worse, and I grieved for Mary for when they crucified her son, Jesus. Instead of taking my son's life, they were trying to save it. I said to the Lord, "Thank you, Lord Jesus, for allowing me to see and sense that."

Ultimately, it became too overwhelming, so, I left the room. I needed some air, prayer, and to go and be with my other loved ones, who were sitting in the waiting room, while the professionals did what they needed to do. Besides, my son was having another breathing episode, which began to make me feel somewhat anxious once again.

During the next few crucial days, while waiting for him to take a significant turn for the better, I wanted to pass the time by making sure they all knew who Sammy was because, up to this point, they only knew him as "fighting for his life in a coma" kind of person. They did not know his personality. He was charming, lovable, witty, sharp, and full of life, but he still liked to tease, like when he was little. If he did not speak to or tease a person, he must have been terribly busy or something. So, I would tell them stories and show them pictures. I would hold my phone up in front of their face and say: "See! That is Sammy right here, the real Sam." I would tell them this was a specific date, and what he was saying and doing. Those poor people probably heard the same stories and seen the same pictures and videos a thousand times, but they were exceedingly kind about it and would laugh as I would gloat. Then, they would comfort me when I would cry, tell me positive things they were seeing, and tell me it was in God's hands. I just loved it when they would say that. I found great comfort in that because I knew it was, but with my emotions I would just need to be reminded and I was so thankful they knew that as well.

John 19:25 (KJV) 25Now there stood by the cross of Jesus his mother, and his mother's sister, Mary the wife of Cleophas, and Mary Magdalene.

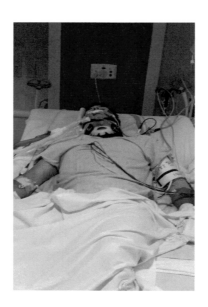

My view while getting the measurements needed

Chapter 10   The God That Heals

Just outside the waiting room, I see my two oldest grandchildren, Gabe, and Navy. That was a precious sight after all the things I had just been viewing. Their sweet little faces, smiles, and hugs just melted my heart. I know I looked worn down, but I hugged them and smiled, and with tears rolling down my cheeks, I asked them to come on with me and pray for Uncle Sammy right then. They shook their little heads yes, and we three bowed our heads, closed our eyes, clasped our hands together, and began to pray. I started with, "Dear Lord Jesus, we need you right now. We need you to heal Uncle Sam. We need a miracle at this very moment, please, Lord. Bring the doctor in fast; it does not look good!"

As I pleaded with the Lord, I could hear my oldest granddaughter, Navy, pleading with Jesus, too. So, I opened my eyes to peek at her and see what my grandson, Gabe, was doing. He had his hands all folded together while he prayed silently. But my granddaughter was just pouring her little heart out to Jesus. She was speaking repeatedly, in a soft whisper, with such great faith and zeal, saying, "Come, Lord Jesus, Please Lord Jesus, Come, Lord Jesus, Please Lord Jesus."

I was just in awe. I knew if Jesus were to hear anything, it would be the plea of these little children with their childlike faith. Let me tell you, she knew how to pray to get results. My oldest daughter, Randi, is their mother. She had gone into Sams's room when I came out. Unknowingly to all of us, we were praying at that exact moment as she was praying over Sam. Wow! After we were finished and said amen, my granddaughter was tugging on my shirt and said to me, "Grandma, I saw him walk in front of us." In a very calm manner, I say to her, "Okay, that's a good thing." We were praying for a doctor, and he came to the rescue. That was fast, too. I had pictured the doctor returning like every other doctor, every additional time they had been doing all along, but I would soon find out that this time was different. After a prompting from the Holy Spirit, I thought for a second, and then asked her, "Wait a minute, who did you see walk by?" She answers so assuredly, "Jesus, grandma"! He walked by right before us while we were praying, and you know what else? He didn't even have to push the button to open the doors. He just walked through them and went to Uncle Sammy room." To explain, you had to press the automatic button so the doors would open. Jesus did not need to push any button and did not need to open any door. He walked right through the closed doors. He was the door that needed to be opened.

So, okay, my eyes were huge, my ears were full, my mind was racing, and I believed her. Don't ever doubt when a child sees into the spiritual realm. I told the kiddies to come with me to Sammy room to see what might be occurring. As we approached the doorway to his room, something strange was happening. Nothing! No doctors were running in and out scurrying along, and the nurses' station was like business as usual. Now, this was not the scene when I had left a few short minutes prior and not the kind of scene any other time those same episodes had arisen with him. So, I stopped to ask the nurse what was happening before I entered the room. I said, "Excuse me! But is everything okay? Is he doing okay? Why is everything so quiet, so calm?" She looked at me very peculiarly and answered, "Yes, everything is fine; he is resting peacefully."

My oldest daughter, Randi was walking out the door as I was walking in. I was telling my daughter what had just happened. She was also surprised and in awe, knowing she had been praying at the same time. I was astonished when I walked in and seen the peace that was over Sammy. We repeatedly asked my granddaughter what she had seen to verify. She would sigh as she was noticeably annoyed and losing her patience with us, saying, "I told you already." Then, she would repeat the same testimony every time. We finally stopped asking her as we did not want her to try to put it out of her mind. My daughter did get the opportunity to ask her what Jesus looked like, and she told her that He looked like He did when he went down to hell.

We understood that to mean in His glorified body when He had defeated death. Victorious. A conqueror. He had just done the same thing with Sammy condition. He conquered the spirit of death that had its grip on him. The devil tripped him up, but God was turning it around for His glory and our good. He brought His peace and healing power into the situation and blanketed Sammy with it. Except for a couple of times, Sammy condition started getting noticeably better.

So, to clear some things up, I want you to know that there were always doctors rushing into the ICU, and at first, this is what I thought my granddaughter was saying. Still, I remembered that I didn't see nor hear anyone walking in front of us, but then I just thought, well, my eyes were closed most of the time while we were praying, so maybe that is why I did not see anyone. Then I realized that she would not have known if this someone were a doctor. Well, a doctor showed up; it was our mighty physician, Jehovah Rapha, our "Mighty Healer," Jesus Christ.

Later, I realized that seeing my son Sammy as Mary saw her son Jesus and the powerful prayer of my granddaughter that caused Jesus to show up was the shift we needed. There was an enormous amount of healing in that moment. Praise the Lord!

John 14:13-14 (KJV) 13 And whatsoever ye shall ask in my name, that will I do, that the Father may be glorified in the Son. 14 If ye shall ask any thing in my name, I will do it.

Chapter 11   Nitric Oxide

The Lord continued to answer my questions because what happened next was just more confirmation for me that my granddaughter had indeed seen Him and what He looked like. He was there to conquer death and heal all for His glory and our good. The Lord had previously told me that and He was showing up and making good on His promise.

After they administered the drug to calm him down, it became more of a waiting game. Just continuously watching, praying, reading scripture, answering texts, visiting visitors, doctors, nurses, and phone calls. It's all a waiting game but producing patience. Even though he had fallen ill with pneumonia, which I had previously mentioned, I knew that the Lord was still healing.

This is when they made the decision to hook him up to Nitric Oxide. It is a gas administered to newborns in the NICU (neonatal unit for underdeveloped lungs). They told me it would be a 50/50 shot because it would work immediately or not at all and that we would know at once like, within seconds. So, this is where it gets good. While standing at the foot of his bed, once again, I was anxiously observing as they hooked him up to a nitric oxide tank. I was incredibly nervous, so I started repeatedly saying the Lord's prayer, just wanting to focus on Jesus and not the situation. I asked the Lord to please let it work. At first I noticed Sammy breathing slowing down and I was a little frightened. I asked one of the respiratory therapists, that was watching and waiting with me, what was happening. Why had his breathing changed so drastically? He looked at me with a big smile, and said, "This is a good thing." I responded, "It is?" He said, "Oh yes, it is." Once again, Jesus proved faithful. The gas worked immediately, and the doctors were smiling and cheering; we all were. I finally understood it to be a great thing and his lungs had a chance to heal. After the encounter with Jesus, I must say he continued to improve supernaturally along with the help of miracle workers sent by Him. Everything they knew to try would end up being the right thing. The Lord was guiding and empowering the doctors every procedure of the way, whether they knew it or not, but personally believe that they did. Thank you Lord.

Romans 5:3-5(KJV) 3And not only so, but we glory in tribulations also: knowing that tribulation worketh patience; 4And patience, experience; and experience, hope: 5And hope maketh not ashamed; because the love of God is shed abroad in our hearts by the Holy Ghost which is given unto us.

Chapter 12   Life Support

I had lived in Sammy ICU room for the duration of his stay. The days had been woefully long before he started improving. Before Jesus was asked to show up by my granddaughter. But during that period of time and while watching Sammy rest, I was keeping my eyes on the life support machine. Looking at and listening to it rise and fall as it was breathing for him, I would pray and read scripture over him. Every night, I listen to it while trying to fall asleep. It was pretty much impossible not to hear it. I can still, in my mind, hear it and all of the machines. The repeated puffs of air from the ventilator, nerve-wracking beeps from the IV monitor, blood pressure and heart vitals machine's alarms. Not being able to sleep because of the obvious, I grew weary. The absurdity of these things being essential for lifesaving measures, then, at the same time, I had come to detest them. Nevertheless, Sammy was improving but displaying no signs of waking up.

I crunched a ton of crushed ice, I read lots of scripture in these hours, and the doctors would come in periodically to give me a prognosis and let me know every update they had uncovered. There wasn't much to reveal except the discussion of removing his life support because he had remained stable for a certain amount of time, and that was a whole other experience to watch and feel.

So, after about three weeks, they shut off the machine, but they did not leave it off because this first time was only a trial run. I watched intently. I was a bundle of nerves, all shaky and sweaty palms. Waiting for Sammy to take the first breath on his own seemed like an eternity, but it was only a matter of a few seconds. When he finally did, his chest expanded as he inhaled in on his own. I watched it go up and down, and it was glorious. Another time of celebration, I was praising Jesus and thinking, why was I so worried?

Genesis 2:7 (KJV) And the LORD God formed man of the dust of the ground and breathed into his nostrils the breath of life; and man became a living soul.

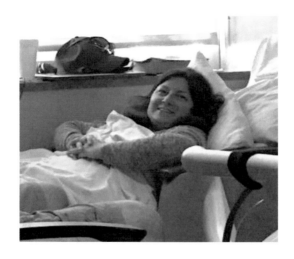

My bed in Sammy's ICU room

Chapter 13   Alone with Jesus

My whole world shook, and everyone knew that. One of the nurses had been recommending that I take pictures and keep a journal and I had been doing that. Another staff member, a female intern that was remarkable at recommending solutions to possibly help, was also telling me the same thing. As I was already writing things down on scattered papers, this intern had purchased a journal for me. I was very thankful and grew to be a little more organized, but there was an urgency for me to document it all. I now realize who guided these people to encourage me to do this: Jesus! The journaling would continue because once he breathed on his own, it reached new levels of praise, awes, excitement and of course healing.

After a few days of taking him off of life support, it was the end of the third week. The doctors had told me that Sammy had finished with ICU, and they were talking about moving him to another room. They informed me that his lying there, breathing independently but not waking up, was probably all the improvement we would see from him. They had seen this kind of thing many times, and this was no different. At first, I just hung my head in grief and disbelief. Again, I believed there was no way the Lord would leave him to lie there like that, not after all the miracles He had performed. I would not accept it. I walked over to my husband with tears rolling down my cheeks, handed him what was in my hands, and said, "I'm going down to the chapel, I need to pray." He said, "I could pray right there." and I said, "I know I can, but this time, I need to be alone with the Lord."

So, I left the room, and as I walked down the hall on my way to the chapel, I could not wait until I got there to bring my burdens to Jesus. So, as I walked the halls to the chapel my talk went like this, "Lord, I will still love you if you decide to take him (my son). I do understand, but please, Lord, if he has not surrendered his life to you (not going to heaven) give him another chance, and please, Lord, don't leave him lay there like that, like a vegetable (lifeless)."

I am sure people watched and listened to me pray as I was walking, but I did not care. In the moment of grief, normally, you don't care about your surroundings. When I arrived at the chapel, it was empty, and I just went straight up to the altar, dropped to my knees, and then face-planted into my hands and on down to the floor I went. I had given everything I had in me, and there was nothing left. I completely surrendered it to Jesus. I begged, cried, and pleaded, please, Lord Jesus! Please do not leave him like that! Please give him another chance! I got up from the floor, dusted myself off, straightened my clothes, grabbed a tissue, wiped off my eyes and face, and headed back upstairs. I felt so much better after crying out, as I always do. That is what the Lord wants us to do; we are not to go through this life and these valleys alone without Him. Thank God!

Isaiah 43:19 (KJV) Behold, I will do a new thing; now it shall spring forth, shall ye not know it? I will even make a way in the wilderness, and rivers in the desert.

James 5:16 (KJV) Confess your faults to one another, and pray one for another, that ye may be healed. The effectual fervent prayer of a righteous man availeth much.

Chapter 14   Where Have You Taken Him?

Sammy was not there when I returned to his room (2nd floor). My son and the bed he was in was gone. His things were also gone. I had just heard a word on peace from Jesus, and they had told me they wanted to move him to another room, but now my human brain went to the question, "Did he die? Is this the peace He meant? Can you imagine my concern? All of this, forgetting that they were moving him upstairs. I frantically asked the nurse on duty, "Where have you taken my son?." She answered, "He is on his way to the 4th floor, to his new room."

So, I walked to the stairwell and went up to the 4th floor. When I arrived at the desk, I told the staff who I was and who I was looking for. The nurse told me Sammy room number, so I went to his room. Almost instantly, as I walked in, he woke up! His eyes opened, and I could not believe mine. I was astonished. We had been waiting on this event for so long, and my prayer brought to my remembrance, and I knew Jesus was still on the scene. He did not leave him like that. He had not forsaken him or my prayers for him because He had opened Sammy eyes. How miraculous! He is a faithful and an awesome God!

While in his new room, however, I would get a little distraught because there were still moments of sadness or heartbrokenness over his condition. Maybe a part of me was so used to receiving grim news I was always trying to emotionally prepare for it. Maybe because even though he had opened his eyes, and I was incredibly grateful for that, he still needed to speak to us. He still needed to walk and eat and recognize us. So many emotions were rolling through my inner being. The Lord had answered my plea for my son in a matter of minutes. But now I asked, "Would Sammy remember me?" Indeed, since the Lord had answered half of the prayer, He would not stop there.

So, as the speech, physical, and respiratory therapists were working with Sammy (trying to help him sit up, eat, drink, and walk), I would sit there waiting for the unavoidable question that would come up, and it finally did. I am referring to the question of who he may recognize. When they sat him up on the edge of the bed, Sammy had an odd look on his face, like he was dizzy, dazed, or confused, which he was all of. Watching it all caused my heart to break for him. I thought he had done nothing to deserve any of this, and I could see the long road ahead of him. I was so grieved, as a mom, when I watched my perfect son struggling to understand reality. The shape of his face was different. What was going on and why, I asked myself. Of course, I was waiting for him to look at me, recognize me, and talk to me. To say momma bear like he always did prior. By this time, I had not really communicated with him for four weeks, and when they asked him if he knew anyone in the room, he was trying to look around to see if he recognized anyone, and then they asked him, "Do you see your mom, Sam?" He replied with a smirk and a gesture of nodding yes and pointing his finger at me. I could have exploded with relief, and I did, with tears. The things I was wanting so badly were breaking me down. I broke down and walked out of the room. I did not want him to see me like that.

Was I grateful or upset? I could not understand what was happening to me. When I left the room and began roaming the halls tears streaming uncontrollably. It felt like a very lonely place. Why was I so broken-hearted and elated that he recognized me? The very idea that he had even opened his eyes. So grateful but so sad he was not talking to us and was not able to walk or eat on his own. I had to be alone with the Lord once again. I asked Him why Sammy was still so messed up. Why was he not like he was before? How long before this nightmare would be over? Thinking, I did not have the strength and courage to continue this journey. The mind and emotions can do terrible things to you. I could not see the end result then, only what was in front of me. Then the Lord steps in, converses with me, and reminds me of things He has already told me, shown me, and promised me. He encourages us and strengthens us to go on in these times. He reminded me of these words of wisdom. "Look at all Sammy has gone through; surely you can go through this?" "Surely you can stay beside him and encourage him?" "Now, go back into that room and watch what I will do."

I felt foolish after that walk and talk. The Lord was right, as always. Indeed, I could be there in Sams's struggles when he needs me the most. I thought, stop being a baby; your son needs you. He needs your help. He needs you to be strong for him. He was in a situation he could not just physically walk away from like you can. He needs your prayers. He still needs you to read scripture over him. So, I did an about-face and marched right back into that room and faced that fear of him possibly never being the same again but prayed for 100% recovery regardless. Thank God I did! Thank God others did. Thank God for God. Thank God for His "still small voice" that told me to go back. Every day that passed, Sammy excelled in healing despite his condition. Only Almighty God can do that!

Isaiah 40:29 (KJV) 29 He giveth power to the faint; and to them that have no might he increaseth strength. 31 Even the youths shall faint and be weary, and the young men shall utterly fall: 31But they that wait upon the LORD shall renew their strength; they shall mount up with wings as eagles; they shall run, and not be weary; and they shall walk, and not faint.

Hebrews 4:16 (KJV) Let us therefore come boldly unto the throne of grace, that we may obtain mercy, and find grace to help in time of need.

James 5:16 (KJV) Confess your faults one to another, and pray one for another, that ye may be healed. The effectual fervent prayer of a righteous man availeth much.

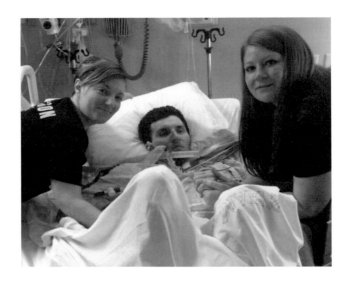

Sammy is awake with sisters (Randi-left/Kensi-right)

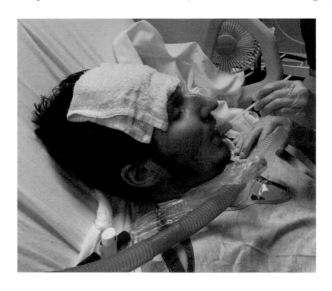

Sammy is awake and getting his teeth cleaned

Chapter 15   Music To My Ears

The following morning, the doctor took the trachea out of Sammy's throat and replaced it with a voice box. Then he leaned over the bed railing, looking down at Sammy, he introduced himself. After that, the doctor told him where he was and why and then said he had been treating him for his injuries. He then explained to Sammy that he would insert a voice box so he could talk. After inserting, he asked, "Can you tell us your name?" There it was, another defining moment we had all been waiting for was to see if he could still talk to us, remember his name, and remember us. So, he responded without flaw and hesitation, "Sammy Cooper."

Oh, Lord! The whole room began rejoicing, jumping, hugging, yelling hooray, hallelujahs, and streaming tears of joy. I know I threw my arms in the air and yelled, "YES!" "Praise Jesus." It was indeed a miracle and music to my ears. I was so happy, to say the least, because no words could have ever described how I was feeling. However, he still had some obstacles that long journey of rehab ahead of him. But regardless, things were now looking even more positive.

The rest of his stay at the emergency facility would only be less than a week before we would move on to rehab #1. The doctors were ready to send Sammy on to this next rehab, but they did not have a bed prepared for him there yet, so we waited another week. The stronger he became, the more aware he became. He was aware that he had a port in his chest with wires hooked to it to read vitals, and he continuously unplugged them. He had an oxygen sensor on his finger that he would not leave on. They moved it to his toes, and he didn't leave it on there, either. The scariest one was the trach in the hole of his throat. He would flick that out when he thought no one was looking. Thankfully, we could just put it back in and tell him to leave it there because he needed it. But really, he already knew he did not need it anymore. God knew he didn't need it anymore as well. It was there for preventive measures, according to the doctors.

The surgeon would need to take it out, stitch the hole together, and it was scheduled it for the following day.

I noticed how his personality was starting to wake up and shine through. It would only be a matter of time for total healing and to God be all the glory.

Philippians 4:4 (KJV) Rejoice in the Lord alway: and again I say, Rejoice.

Chapter 16   The Bridge I Named Faith

Finally, after a week on the 4th floor and scarcely teaching him to eat, drink, and talk because he had just barely gained consciousness, time was closing in on the move to #1 Rehab Center.

The feeling of being unable to bring Sammy home was a little disappointing, but I had been recharged with hope even though this still meant weeks or even months of rehab ahead of us. While driving to our next destination, we first needed to stop by our home and gather some more belongings. Something I had been dreading was that on the same path to my home, we would be crossing the bridge of the accident site. The bridge that Sammy had fallen from, the bridge I named Faith.

So, as we approached the bridge, I was very emotional, with tears rushing down my cheeks, and it was hair-raising to see the railroad tracks below and how far of a drop it was. It nearly sent me into a panic attack. The fatal tracks that took my son's life. Our world would never again be the same traveling through this area like when I was younger. We drove that road to my grandmother's house, but now it was a dreadfully different memory altogether. It was useless when I tried to look away; my thoughts and eyes were too nosey. I wanted to see if I could even draw a picture in my mind's eye with great detail of what happened there. It felt like some closure for me, I guess. I understood the "need to know" about how loved ones feel without closure. I have yet to meet the wonderful woman who saw the fall and flagged down the police officer. I did have one opportunity to speak with her over a phone conversation, and she said that she, too, had a son who was 23 years old. That had to be very traumatizing to her as well, as I found out she was not yet ready to talk about what she had witnessed. I don't know, and I may never know if it was because she was thinking about me emotionally, her own emotions, or maybe both. It would have been very therapeutic for me, though, and I pray she will share someday.

I had the opportunity to meet the police officer who she had flagged down. I have not met the first responders and the initial staff that was on duty at the ER at the hospital before the life flight, but right after the accident happened. I know I would love it too eventually.

The bridge is more than just something vehicles use to cross; it is where faith began for many, where faith expounded supernaturally, and where faith is what it took to make a miracle happen. I have chosen to see it as a place of holiness, courage, mercy, and grace, a place of a new life as long as I keep my eyes on Jesus. If I look away, I could remain in the sad thoughts, and believe me, I have at times, but when I shift my focus to the miracle at the prompting of the Holy Spirit, I am in awe, thinking about what all spiritually took place there—hearing what witnesses that would speak with me, was almost like seeing it myself. So detailed and full of emotion. It helped me visualize and realize the tragedy's magnitude and fill in some gaps. I am immensely grateful for so many who stepped up to testify. This is why I needed to hear it from them as I still do.

Upon arrival at my home, I was a bit shaky. Everything was different from 4 weeks earlier and a little surreal. I was also still wondering about how my son was doing as I was concerned about leaving him, but I knew I had to get to the 1st Rehab Center to get him checked into his room, and us checked into ours. And another thing, Sammy had to fly there, and that kept me nervous. I was home for one night; we departed from there the next afternoon, June 30th. It was about a two-and-a-half-hour drive from my hometown, and we were exhausted. Everything from the past four weeks had taken a toll, and the journey was not even half over.

Matthew 11:28-30 (KJV) 28 Come unto me, all ye that labour and are heavy laden, and I will give you rest. 29 Take my yoke upon you, and learn of me; for I am meek and lowly in heart: and ye shall find rest unto your souls.

Chapter 17   God's Sense of Humor

Before I discuss what arriving at the hotel entailed, little did I know that Sammy dad and I were to become roommates for four weeks when our journey landed us in the first rehab facility. Everyone just thought we were together, like married, together. They would talk to us assuming it because that is how it appeared to them. We had to stay in the same hotel room because they would only furnish one for the whole family. I am grateful I didn't have to pay for it out of my pocket, but I thought, really, God! I am not finding this the least bit funny, but God was raining grace on us, and at least we were able to be around one another without feelings of bitterness. We needed that to get through this without more wounds and scars. Fast forward to now, but looking back to then, it is pretty humorous. We spent almost five weeks in the same room as exes and survived. We would stop by this unique café every morning for breakfast on our walk to the rehab building. Only God could submerge us with the grace needed to live with an ex, even for an hour, and this turned into weeks. Honestly, we just concentrated on the recovery of our son, and so it was one day at a time. We were there for him.

So, back to arriving at the big city and locating our hotel, we pulled up in front of it. My husband and youngest son carried our things in, and I followed behind them. To let you know, I was born and raised in a small town. Actually, on the outskirts of a small town, this big city thing was immediately not setting well with me similar to how elevators feel to me. I had more elevators; this time, it was not two or four floors but seven. Okay, now the Lord will have to pull off another miracle here, and I was not trying to be ungrateful, but it was elevators; I highly dislike them, as I said earlier. After talking with the desk clerk, we worked out a deal that I could use the stairs, but they kept it locked on the first floor, and they would have to let me in, but it would open from inside the stairwell, and I immediately struck that deal. It kept me out of the elevator. Thank you, Jesus! They were fire escapes, and they were very dim, creepy, and entirely of concrete. I often wondered if they were worse than the elevators, laughing at myself here.

We finally got to the room and got our rough first night's sleep. Then, we awoke with another long day ahead of us. I wanted to be home, but I was not letting my son go through with this alone. I mean, how could I? I love him so much; I am a mom and God already had that talk with me.

The following day, when we arrived at the #1 rehab center, it was another tall building with 16 floors. It was the same scenario with the elevator and stairs, so I would need to use them. They thought I was ridiculous and asked me why I didn't just take the elevator. I, of course, told them, "I do not do elevators." So, the security guard agreed to escort me to the 9th floor whenever I would need him to. That was the floor Sammy was on for the first week, and then for the two weeks, I climbed up to the 10th floor because the last two weeks, I ended up taking the elevators after all. Again, laughing at myself here. I trusted the Lord to get me up and down for the rest my stay. He was good on His promise because there was not one issue. Day and night, I walked to the rehab building and then again back to the motel room, which was about 7 to 10 big city blocks, and I was getting very exhausted. However, the exercise was good for me, and I knew I would be there for a while and to draw on His strength. Ultimately, I was in the best shape I had been in for a long time.

There were many days of the same questions, the same answers, different doctors' diagnoses, other therapist's same therapies, and constant monitoring. It took a toll on me mentally and emotionally, but I knew I needed to press on. I knew my son was in a much worse condition than I was. He was going through physical and emotional therapy every day, also. Starting with the physical disadvantage then he was the one trapped in the brain injury, trying to remember his life again. He was the one with double vision and being evaluated constantly. Even after all he had been through, he felt glad it had happened to him because he was the only one who was not married nor had any kids. I broke down with tears when he said that. I was so proud of his sacrificial heart. I told him that I would not have it happen at all, but to envision any child or loved one to have to visit their father in that condition would have been devastating to any family. I had to agree with him, with an aching, bittersweet heart, and for any child's sake, this was the "better" option.

Now, for some good news. Sam, once again, started improving rapidly. He was beginning to remember very well and started eating normally. Finally, he was able to tie his shoes again. Getting into the bathroom and back to bed. He was doing so well that at the end of his fourth week, he was breezing through all the exercises and activities that the doctors wanted to transfer him to rehab #2. Again, for the second time, I was informed of the need to wait one more week for a room to open up. The good news was his improvement, so the bad news of waiting didn't matter or even seem like bad news. Besides, it is all on God's time anyway.

2 Peter 3:8 (KJV) But, beloved, be not ignorant of this one thing, that one day is with the Lord as a thousand years, and a thousand years as one day.

Front-Sammy's father (Gary) and I

Left-Sammy Right-Chace (younger brother)

Chapter 18　No More Elevators

Departing once again, Sammy went by airplane, and my husband, my youngest son, and I traveled by car. Leaving the big city was a breath of fresh air. As I stared into the side view mirror, the city was disappearing, and the farther away we drove from it, the more relaxed I was. I had a lot of time to reflect on everything that had happened, and I once again broke down crying. After all, there was yet another transition, and I was trying to grasp where we would fit in when we returned home.

Arriving at rehab #2, I was relieved to see we were on solid ground. No elevators or dark and creepy stairwells. Sammy had physical and occupational therapy several days a week. Sometimes, it was rough on him, but it helped to strengthen him overall. We would take him places to see how well he would function in the world, like having him create a grocery list and take him shopping to gather and buy the items. They would have him figure his finances and teach him organizational skills. We took him golfing; he even hunted and snagged a deer with a bow and arrow. They had him involved in a woodworking class, where he built a bookcase. He rode special bikes and planned, prepared, and cooked meals. He went on the lake in a boat. We went to a rodeo, which was the first time I had been to one; it was exciting. We even found a church to attend for our duration there.

Sammy had to go through many tests to make sure he could drive again and go to work again. He had to see a psychiatrist to be sure he was mentally stable to be out in society and have typical relationships. Overall, he was highly functional, so another praise for the Lord!

Thankfully, I had my brand-new family housing unit right across the street from Sam. It was all free for me because some exceptional people funded it. Truly a huge blessing!

After 2-1/2 months there, we headed for home, but Sammy had to do a test run back to work. He passed, so he was released for that. He had many follow-up appointments, which can be very inconvenient, and a drastic change from where he had been, praise God still!

Psalm 26:12 (NIV) My feet stand on level ground; in the great congregation I will praise the Lord.

Chapter 19   An Unknown Prayer Warrior

I would later discover an elderly lady at my in-law's church who was praying for Sam. She was an unknown prayer warrior to us and my in-laws but only known to the Holy Spirit. While reading the newspaper headlines, she found the article about Sammy accident and led to cut his picture out of the newspaper and keep it lying on her table so she could lay her hands on it and pray daily for this young man she did not even know. So, there was no way she could see the connection. Also, she had not seen or heard of any updates on him, but still, she would keep praying. We would later take Sammy to meet her one Sunday, she told us that she did not know he was a step grandson to my in-laws and was quite astonished when that was revealed to her and everyone else in the congregation. She explained how enlightened she was to see the part she had played in this testimony and so happy she was to be able to meet him in person. Only God knew, and yet, another miracle happened!

Ephesians 6:18 (NIV) 18And pray in the Spirit on all occasions with all kinds of prayers and requests. With this in mind, be alert and always keep on praying for all the Lord's people.

Chapter 20   The Return To The Bridge

In September 2016, we made a quick trip back home because Sammy was to take part in a close friend's wedding. We made a surprise stop at the emergency facility, where Sammy was life-flighted to by helicopter. We decided to do this so Sammy could meet the people who took such great care of him and personally thank them. Since he was in a coma most of the duration there, he did not remember anyone. Also, we wanted to show them how miraculous he was doing to praise Jesus. They were all so grateful to know that we cared so much to visit them. They take remarkable care of their patients and care so much, and I believe they are often forgotten about when the dust settles. They said, "Witnessing his recovery encourages them to continue their actions for others." It makes it all worth it because, more often than not, a tragic situation of this scale does not turn into a miracle like this. They say they do their job, but they all went above and beyond. In the end, they were extremely grateful that we visited.

One of the nurses that cared for Sammy jumped on the opportunity while hugging me, with tears in her eyes and a lump in her throat to whisper in my ear, "You received your miracle." I agreed, nodding my head while saying "Yes," with tears streaming down, and we engaged in another embrace.

After visiting the staff who played a huge role in caring for Sammy, we stopped by the doctor's office that had treated Sammy lungs. He was so happy to see how well Sammy was doing like the staff had also been. Just knowing he did his job and worked tirelessly to save Sammy life and the miraculous outcome was highly gratifying to him. We took some pictures along the way and will soon include them in the back pages of the book.

From there, we drove to the bridge where the tragedy happened. Since I was not there when it happened, no one who had witnessed it was there with us, and Sammy has no memory, we walked around, trying to visualize the scene as it had played out. It was surreal. I was envisioning, to the best of my ability, from what I had heard from the first-hand witnesses, what it may have looked like him lying dead on the railroad tracks below the bridge. I was standing on the tracks, just staring down at them. Though It was on more pleasant terms because of his healing and as he had no memory of the fall. Part of the healing process is moving forward and maybe having some closure.

He was curious to see if maybe it might spark a memory. It didn't do that, but what a trooper, he "got back on that horse." I was immensely proud of and happy for him. To go back there where he had fallen to his death and not with a second thought or faintness of a reaction.

It was a special moment with a supernatural awe at The Bridge of Faith.

Philippians 4:13 (KJV) "I can do all things through Christ which strenghteneth me."

Sammy and I (TK Hinkle - mother)

The tracks where Sammy landed

Chapter 21   A Brand-New Life

Several years have passed since my son's accident. However, the taste and smell of the tragedy are still extraordinarily fresh in my life, in my memory, in my family, in my being, and forever will be. However, the presence of Jesus is compelling.

In the end, JESUS gets all of the praise and glory. He performed many miracles, and my son walks, talks, eats, and breathes independently. The life he lives is different now as there are some hurdles, but it could have been worse. He still works in the same career field where he plans to retire.

He now has a baby girl who is two years of age, and that would not have been possible if the Lord had not spared his life. This new little life would not have existed if the Lord had allowed that generation to pass. Hallelujah! Sammy loves and adores his daughter; she loves and adores him, and she makes his heart happy and full. This accident has enabled him to see how precious life is and how quickly it can change. We recently traveled back to where The Bridge of Faith is, and we took Sammy daughter with us. She repeated, "Daddy fall" the rest of the trip. I think it is a positive thing to let her know what happened to her daddy, as she is a tremendous part of his continued recovery.

Thank you, Jesus!

Revelation 2:15 (KJV) "And he that sat upon the throne said, Behold, I make all things new, And he said unto me, Write: for these words are true and faithful."

Sammy and his daughter (Kaislea)

Chapter 22   Encouragement

Every day, as I watched the chest tubes flow bloody liquid from Sammy's body and drip into a bag that they would need to empty, I also watched as they put in new IV meds used to keep him fed and comfortable and then ultimately a medically induced coma. Then, as I mentioned earlier, no matter how hard they tried to prevent it, he ended up with pneumonia and needed an IV for antibiotics. Thank God something could be done to help all of his issues.

I could not imagine this becoming an everyday life occurrence. I would not imagine it or accept it. I decided to do just that, to say no; this would never be the "norm." The Lord gave me enough proof, hope, strength, and faith to know that He was working a miracle in Sammy's body and mind. Although it wasn't always easy on my emotions because there were times when some would try to sway me from believing God's promises, but I did hang on to God has the final say.

I want to make a note to the caretakers. I have met many fantastic people along this journey and am thankful. My son's wonderful nurse at rehab#2. Turned out that she was a Christian. I could testify to her of Jesus' miracles in Sammy's situation. So many need to hear of it to build hope, faith, strength, edification, and encouragement.

The Lord may have very well spared my son's life, and I am eternally grateful for that; my journey through this tragedy, no matter how one views it, was still that of heartbreak, heartache, shell shock, and ups and downs. I still have occasional sad flashbacks that surface, knowing of his struggles through everyday life challenges and knowing it has not been, nor will it be a breeze in this life post-accident.

Even though Sammy has seemingly walked away unscathed, the tragedy would leave our family forever emotionally scared and changed. Trials are challenging because they are refining. I knew my relationship with JESUS would be all I needed if I stayed believing. But I wonder about others. What and who are they putting their faith and belief in? We are truly fortunate to have knowledge and understanding of the truths in the bible. JESUS always has our back just by trusting in Him. He has us covered spiritually and mentally as well when we trust Him. I had His word to turn to and meditate on and renew my mind daily, but it doesn't mean the feelings and emotions won't rise out of the flesh occasionally. They are rough! They do not quickly subside, but it is not impossible; God makes all things possible. Our flesh (mind, will, and emotions) wants to win. So, at times they can just be more problematic for us.

I am incredibly grateful to say that through all of it, I remained drug and alcohol-free. I did not use any substances for comfort, healing, or masking; only our Lord can give that peace that surpasses all understanding. I am only bragging about Him because, at one time, I did drink alcohol and was supernaturally delivered eight years earlier to 2016, when He took all of the addictions and insane thinking away. I also brag because He is faithful and deserves it. So, I am not criticizing or condemning anyone who needs these as a way of help, it is just not in my life anymore. This is my prayer for you as well. Hoping I am an example of faith, belief, and trust because of my comforter, the Holy Spirit.

In the end, He is all we need, all I needed, and miraculously all Sammy needed. Hallelujah!

Most importantly, I am a vessel for my Lord Jesus Christ. For I am the clay, and He is the potter. He has molded me into what I am today. He has turned up the heat and cured this vessel of clay that can stand up and withstand because of the subject matter poured into it as long as I keep my focus on Him and the word of God. Amen!

Isaiah 64:8 (KJV) But now, Oh Lord, though art our father; we are the clay, and thou are potter; and we all are the work of thy hand.

Ephesians 6:10-18 (KJV) Finally, be strong in the Lord and in his mighty power. Put on the full armor of God, so that you can take your stand against the devil's schemes. For our struggle is not against flesh and blood, but against the rulers, against the authorities, against the powers of this dark world and against the spiritual forces of evil in the heavenly realms. Therefore put on the full armor of God, so that when the day of evil comes, you may be able to stand your ground, and after you have done everything, to stand. Stand firm then, with the belt of truth buckled around your waist, with the breastplate of righteousness in place, And with your feet fitted with the readiness that comes from the gospel of peace. In addition to all this, take up the shield of faith, with which you can extinguish all the flaming arrows of the evil one. Take the helmet of salvation and the sword of the Spirit, which is the word of God. And pray in the Spirit on all occasions with all kinds of prayers and requests. With this in mind, be alert and always keep on praying for all the Lord's people. Ephesians 6:10-18 (NIV)

Scriptures That Gave Me Comfort

Behold, I will do a new thing; now it shall spring forth; shall ye not know it? I will even make a way in the wilderness, and rivers in the desert. Isaiah 43:19 (KJV)

And we know that all things work together for good to them that love God, to them who are the called according to his purpose. Romans 8:28 (KJV)

For the Lord thy God will hold thy right hand, saying unto thee, Fear not; I will help thee. Isaiah 41:13 (KJV)

Jesus said unto him, Thou shalt love the Lord thy God with all thy heart, and with all thy soul, and with all thy mind. Matt. 22:37 (KJV)

And I say unto you, Ask, and it shall be given you; seek, and ye shall find; knock, and it shall be opened unto you. Luke 11:9 (KJV)

And whatsoever ye shall ask in my name, that will I do, that the Father may be glorified in the Son. If ye shall ask any thing in my name, I will do it. John14:13-14 (KJV)

Jesus saith unto him, I am the way, the truth, and the life: no man cometh unto the Father, but by me. John 14:6 (KJV)

Therefore, if anyone is in Christ, the new creation has come: The old has gone, the new is here! 2 Corinthians 5:17 (NIV)

I am the vine, ye are the branches: He that abideth in me, and I in him, the same bringeth forth much fruit: for without me ye can do nothing. John 15:5 (KJV)

But when you ask, you must believe and not doubt, because the one who doubts is like a wave of the sea, blown and tossed by the wind. James 1:6 (NIV)

The Power of God is Working in You and Through You in Jesus's name, Amen

LET'S CHAT FOR A MINUTE

There is only one way to salvation: one way into Heaven! If you are in Christ, He is in you!

Stand firm on what you pray for and keep believing no matter what is before you! We are in a spiritual war. An enemy that we cannot see!

I, TK Hinkle, a believer in Jesus Christ, know that He is Almighty God in the flesh. He shed His sinless blood and died for me so that I am forgiven if I believe and trust this as truth then I would spend eternity with Him in heaven if I so chose to. I have chosen to. I believe He is who He says He is, God in the flesh and that He died for all of the sins of the world.

Let me ask you a question, an especially important question. If you should die today, are you 100% certain that you are going to Heaven?

If you should die today and stand before God, and He asked you why He should let you into His Heaven, what would you say?

Did you know that you can be 100% certain you are going to Heaven? You CAN know, and please read on to learn how.

Romans 3:10 (KJV) As it is written, There is none righteous, no, not one:

Romans 3:23 (KJV) For all have sinned, and come short of the glory of God; That means I'm a sinner, and that means you are a sinner also. Most people do not realize the seriousness of sin. God is holy, and sin separates a sinner from God.

This verse shows how serious it is!

Romans 5:12 (KJV) Wherefore, as by one man sin entered into the world, and death by sin; and so death passed upon all men, for that all have sinned: The word "death" doesn't mean dying and going to the grave; it means separation from God. Unless we believe this truth, we will stay separated from God on this earth, and we will be separated from God forever in a place called Hell.

If my son had stayed dead and did not trust or believe upon the Lord Jesus Christ for eternal life before he died, he would have gone to hell. This is the punishment for our sin, and we do not know if our current breath is our last one and then our life is over forever. Thankfully, he did believe and trust in Him.

But the story doesn't end here!

Romans 6:23 (KJV) For the wages of sin is death; but the gift of God is eternal life through Jesus Christ our Lord. The words "eternal life" mean more than living forever; they mean to live forever in Heaven.

Notice that being saved is a gift—it's absolutely free! You can't buy it, work for it, or be good enough for it. It is free! It would be as if a friend went to the store and bought you a present. They paid for it, wrapped it, put a bow on it, and brought it to you. They did everything for you. All you have to do is receive it.

That is what Jesus did! He left His home in Heaven, came to earth, died on the cross, shed His sinless blood, and paid for your sins. He did everything for you. Again, all you have to do is receive it. Open your heart like you would a present and say thank you! This means that you believe He is Almighty God in the flesh, born of a virgin, shed His sinless blood when He died on the cross. It means you believed/accepted/received His free gift of salvation. *Romans 5:8 (KJV) But God commendeth his love toward us, in that, while we were yet sinners, Christ died for us.*

Most people think they have to stop doing everything bad before God will save them. But God loves us as sinners, and Jesus died for us. When Jesus died for you, He made it possible for you to have forgiveness of sins and eternal life with Him forever.

John 14:6 (KJV) Jesus saith unto him, I am the way, the truth, and the life: no man cometh unto the Father, but by me. However, just because Jesus died for you, that does not automatically save you.

The following questions have **Yes** or **No** answers. Regardless of what your answers are I pray you will choose continuing to read until the end. You will never regret giving your whole heart to Jesus, but you would eventually regret not going to Heaven when you die.

1.) Now, do you admit that you are a sinner?

2.) Do you understand that sin separates you from God?

3.) Do you believe Jesus died on the cross for you and understand why He did this?

4.) Would you like to be forgiven of all your sins and know 100% you are going to Heaven?

If **YES**, then this is what you need to do.

Romans 10:9-13 (KJV) That if thou shalt confess with thy mouth the Lord Jessus, and believe in thine heart that God hath raised him from the dead, thou shalt be saved. For with the heart man believeth unto righteousness; and with the mouth confession is made unto salvation. For the scripture saith, Whosoever believeth on him shall not be ashamed. For there is no difference between the Jew and the Greek: for the same Lord is over all is rich unto all that call upon him. For whosoever shall call upon the name of the Lord shall be saved. Then, according to the Bible, if you asked Jesus into your heart right now, He would save you forever! Wouldn't you like to do this? If you will trust Jesus to take you to Heaven when you die, then just tell Him you believe and trust Him to do that.

I would like to point you to these salvation scriptures before you pray.

1 Corinthians 1:1-4 (KJV) Paul called to be an apostle of Jesus Christ through the will of God, and Sosthenes our brother, Unto the church of God which is at Corinth, to them that are sanctified in Christ Jesus, called to be saints, with all that in every place call upon the name of Jesus Christ our Lord, both their's and our's: Grace be unto you, and peace, from God our Father, and from the Lord Jesus Christ. I thank my God always on your behalf, for the grace of God which is given you by Jesus Christ.

"Dear Jesus, I know I am a sinner. I believe You are the Almighty God of Abraham, Issac, and Jacob in the flesh. You were born of a virgin, and You died for my sins and came alive from the dead. Thank you for dying for me and forgiving me for all of my sins. I believe and trust you will come into my heart right now and you will give me a home forever in Heaven when I die. Thank you for the Holy Spirit to Help me and to guide all of my steps. I mean this prayer with all my heart! Amen."

If you have done this, then according to the Bible, you are saved—and if you were to die today, you would go to Heaven!

I also want to encourage you to:

1.) Read the Bible so that you can grow in your faith—maybe start with Colossians, then Romans, and Corinthians next. After that you will have a deeper understanding of who Christ is. Paul was the apostle to the Gentiles, which by definition is, if you are not a Jew, then you are a Gentile.

To help you to learn more about the Bible, I suggest you also go to www.BibleHub.com.

2) Pray to God—He cares for you. Jesus gives an example of how to pray in *Matthew 6:9-13.*

3) Find a Bible-based church—one that not only teaches the Bible but will help you to grow in your faith.

4) Paul gives us an explanation for water baptism in *Romans 6:4 (KJV) Therefore we are buried with him by baptism into death: that like as Christ was raised up from the dead by the Father, even so we also should walk in the newness of life.*

Acknowledgment and Perspectives

I (TK Hinkle) am penning this testimony for my Lord Jesus. This miracle was not only a result of a tragic circumstance in my life, my son's life, and my entire family's life, but an event that has forever altered all of our lives. I want everyone to see the Lord's kindness, goodness, and overwhelming unconditional love for us all. Ingrained into my mind, heart, and soul, it is very emotional for me, for I have not quickly forgotten, and I do not take it for granted. But most importantly, I am a vessel for my Lord Jesus Christ. God's power, miracles, and saving grace, and His purpose is for and through our lives. May your hearts be responsive to the love of Jesus.

– TK Hinkle (mother)

On May 29th, 2016, I cooked chicken on my grill for our family picnic. It was on Memorial Day, and it was my last memory before my accident. The first memory post-accident was of my roommate at rehabilitation #1. We both had feeding tubes, and he opened the shake in a can he had discovered in the refrigerator. He chugged it down, not knowing he wasn't supposed to, and when the nurse found out, she said it must have tasted terrible. It didn't hurt him, but at least it was a funny memory. I made many friends there and went on a few outings around the town. I remember leaving there and heading to rehabilitation #2. I was worried about going because I had to fly, and I was not too fond of the thought of flying. Also, while at this second rehabilitation, I met many great people who cared about my recovery and a couple of friends with whom I am still occasionally in contact. I did have a fracture in my left wrist,

which I had surgery on and then some rehabilitation for as well. That ended up being a longer process than I thought it would be. But thankfully, I have my wrist, and I can use it. Everyone was trained and equipped to care for me, did a great job, and helped me function again. A few stand out, and I am thankful for everyone. In some ways, it seems like it took forever to go home. In reality, I was back to work after 4 ½ months. That is indeed a short time compared to most injuries like mine, and in many cases, it takes years, if it even happens at all. I now have a daughter, which would not have been possible if God had not healed me. She is my best friend and puts my heart in a happy place. I want to give thanks to everyone who did fundraisers, sent cards, called, visited, and worked overtime to aid in saving my life.
- **Sammy Cooper (the living miracle)**

A phone call woke me up that my brother, Sammy, had been in an accident. Our family didn't know much at the time except that he was being life-flighted. My heart stopped, and time stopped. I frantically ran to wherever in the house, pacing through the house. He arrived at the hospital via an ambulance, and I can't remember many details after that, except that I needed to get hold of the hospital. I made a phone call to that facility and spoke to a nurse who told me that he was being life-flighted to another facility. The nurse also said that the doctors were praying over my brother briefly while he was there. I remember her also saying they were all still praying for him. At this moment, I knew it was probably going to be his final moments and that he was not going to make it by the sound of the nurse's voice and her words. I didn't even need to know the details of the injuries. I just knew it was tragic. My sister, Kensi, and I drove to the hospital my brother had been life-flighted to, and it was an exceptionally long drive. We arrived and were escorted directly to the ICU waiting area. Being escorted just furthered the fear I already had. When we got to the waiting area, I saw my mom and just hugged her. She was in shock as we all were, and looking back, I now know why the hug didn't seem to even register with her.

I wanted to help her with that hug. I wanted a hug, too, as I was deathly afraid I was losing my brother. The details started coming in from everywhere. The news of what had happened. The news from the doctors of what all was wrong with him. It was all too much for me. All I knew to do was pray, and I wanted to see him, knowing it could be the last. It seemed to take forever to get to his room and see him. I barely remember seeing him for the first time because of all the sad and scary emotions.

Prayers reached worldwide over the next few weeks, a miracle. It had been months before the accident since my mom and I had talked. We were not on good terms, and this brought us back together. Looking back, I hate that this incident to open our eyes.

The news after about two weeks was that my brother was going to survive, but we still had a long road ahead; it brought me relief and also, at the same time, grief. Because even though my brother was going to survive, he would never be the same, and I had to grieve the death of the Sammy that was and would be no longer. And try to learn how to embrace the different Sammy he would become. A brain injury changes people, and so it is a death and rebirth at the same time. Being the oldest of five siblings, I always had that sense of protection over them. And this was one thing I could not save him from. Except for the power of prayer and God!

My brother was transported to other facilities as his healing and rehabilitation would require. Unfortunately, I could not be there with him like I wanted so desperately to be. Thankfully, my brother has been restored to life, mentally and physically. I remember telling Sammy while he was in his medically induced coma that he needed to stay with us and that we had some unresolved issues to fix, and he squeezed my hand. He was unhappy with me and had not talked to me since my mother and I were on the outs. I found out that when he squeezed my hand, it was during this time Jesus had walked into Sammy's room. From that day on, he began to improve. I remember telling God. "Lord, please spare his life, and I'll never complain about his pestering behavior again.' "Just bring my brother back, please!"
 – **Randi Milam (oldest sister)**

June 1, 2016, is a day that forever changed my family and my life. That morning, I received a phone call from my grandmother while sleeping. I don't recall the exact time, but it was still early morning. When I answered, she told me that Sammy had been in an accident at work and was life-flighted. I was devastated, shocked, scared, and alone. I called my husband, who was working thousands of miles away, and barely got the news out to him through sobbing cries. When we hung up, I was trying to figure out my next steps. My one-year-old daughter was still sleeping, so I called my sister, Randi. I asked if I could come over, got what I needed for my daughter, and rushed down the road to her house. Randi and I sat at her kitchen table discussing everything, and I knew I needed to call my mom. When she answered, I remember being shocked at her voice's somewhat calmness but also fear. She asked me, "Who was driving? Was Sammy driving when the accident happened?" I said, "What? Mom, Sammy fell from the bridge." I was confused, wondering if I knew what happened to him. She immediately started sobbing and crying uncontrollably, and I was trying to get her to answer me if my stepdad, Chuck, was driving and with her at that moment. She couldn't say anything that made sense. I said, "I don't know what to do," and handed the phone to my sister. She eventually calmed our mom down, and I was still trying to process what was happening. Did he fall from the bridge? Was he in a car accident? Did the truck run off the side of the bridge while driving to work? I decided to call Sammy's dad, Gary, and we found out that Sammy had been life-flighted again to another hospital, and he had confirmed he had fallen from the bridge. My sister, her kids, my daughter, and I headed down south for a 2-hour drive that never ended. I remember people calling us on our way down, other family members, but I can't remember who all it was or what the conversations were. I knew I had to get to the hospital to see Sammy before it was too late. When we arrived at the hospital, a receptionist asked as we were coming in if we were the family of the young man flown in. We answered that we were we must have looked frantic for her to know who we were there for. She said, "I believe he will be okay, they are working on some things, but they are taking care of him." We were very thankful for her, giving us hope that everything would be alright. We finally made it to the waiting room, and I could see my mom standing outside the room, still in her work boots and uniform. I gave her a big hug as we all cried. I looked around to see some of Sammy's coworkers, a couple of business people from his company, family, and friends; we were all waiting to see Sammy. When I was finally able to see Sammy, I had no words.

All I could do was cry. Machines all hooked up to him, tubes coming out of him, his eyes closed, his hands had blood on them, blood on his pillowcase from where his head hit the railroad tracks. I remember looking at him and thinking he is so strong; this can't be the end for him. I grabbed his left hand, crying and praying, pleading for you to live, and I felt his hand squeeze mine back. At that very moment, I felt in my heart and knew he was still with us, fighting for his life, and he wouldn't give up. I had never seen him so fragile; he's always been my strong, big little brother, full of laughs, carefree, and ready to go. For the first time that day, I had a clear sign of life from you and a little relief, a peace that passes all understanding, just like the Bible says. Although I knew there was still a long road ahead of us, God healed my brother.

- Kensi Rader (second oldest sister)

It was morning, and I was still sleeping. My dad woke me up and said, "Get up and get ready. We need to leave; Sammy was in an accident." So, in my mind, I thought Sammy was in a vehicle accident. I was picturing him in his truck wrapped around a tree. When my dad and I arrived at my mother's work and walked in, I went to the restroom around the corner to splash water on my face while looking in the mirror to see if this was all real or a bad dream. I then could hear my dad tell my mom, "Don't freak out!" Next, as I walked up by my dad, I could see my mom's face as she was very distraught, and she was weeping hysterically. She was weak-kneed, and we aided her until she had to gather her things. After a few short minutes, as we headed to the vehicle, I could hear my mom reciting bible verses. The drive to the hospital was almost a three-hour drive. I sat in

the back seat and remember staring out the window almost the whole trip. A couple of times, my mom would turn around, look at me, and ask me to sing with her. So I would. Then, it was back to a continued gaze out the window. Before I knew it, we had arrived where my brother was. Ingrained into my memory is the smell of the inside of the hospital and the sound of all of the machines aiding in my brother's life-saving moments. I felt this heavy weight or intense pressure, causing me to think about never hearing my brother's infectious laugh or talking to him again. Seeing him struggle with every breath just made him look so helpless. Even though all of the hopelessness, seeing his condition failing repeatedly. Even though I thought it was going to be his last breath and hear his last heartbeat, I still prayed for a fast and 100 percent recovery. It did not seem fast for me, but when I felt him squeeze my hand, it boosted my hope, and I was and am still thankful for every second because God showed me his physical healing power.
– **Chace Logan (younger brother)**

Photos

Family Photo

Sammy and Randi (sister)

Sammy, Bill, Karen Hinkle (Grandparents),
and Henli (niece)

Sammy with Kensi (sister)

Pastor Marc, Lisa (wife) and I

Sammy, Gabe (nephew),
Navy, Henli (niece)

Sammy and his daughter (Kaislea)

Sammy and Gary (Father)

Front-Chace (younger brother) and Sammy

Miracles upon Miracles